HOW TO STOP NEGATIVE THINKING

7 Strategies to Help You Stop Negative Thinking as a teenager

Smart Desty

Copyright © [2023], [Smart Desty]

Table of Contents

Introduction

Conclusion

Introduction

Negative thinking is a pattern of thinking that focuses on the downside of situations, perceiving life through a pessimistic lens. It can lead to a host of unhealthy emotions, such as fear, guilt, and sadness. It can also cause physical symptoms such as headaches, stomach problems, and insomnia. Negative thinking can be debilitating and can lead to feelings of hopelessness and despair. It can cause individuals to feel as if they are unable to move forward and that they can never be happy. It can also lead to a lack of motivation and difficulty making decisions. Fortunately, there are several strategies that can help individuals combat negative thinking and create more positive and productive thought patterns.

Negative thinking occurs when an individual interprets situations, events, and people in a negative way and focuses on the worst possible outcome of any given situation. It often involves blaming oneself or externalizing the blame onto others. It can also lead to a cycle of rumination, where individuals continually replay negative thoughts in their head. This can lead to feelings of guilt and shame, as well as self-doubt and a lack of self-confidence. Negative thinking can lead to an inability to trust others, a feeling of being disconnected from the world, and a lack of motivation or ambition.

Negative thinking affects productivity in many ways. It can lead to difficulty concentrating, procrastination, and a lack of productivity. It also has the ability to initiate the feelings of depression, anxiety, and low self-esteem. Additionally, it can lead to unhealthy coping mechanisms, such as alcohol or drugs.

Negative thinking is detrimental to mental and physical health and can prevent individuals from living their best life. It is important to recognize when negative thinking is occurring and to take steps to address it. There are several strategies for combating negative thinking, such as cognitive restructuring, positive self-talk, and mindfulness. It is also important to practice self-care and seek professional help if needed. With the right tools and strategies, it is possible to break free from the cycle of negative thinking and create a more positive outlook.

As a teenager negative thinking also have a huge impact on mental health as young people are prone to anxiety and depression. Negative thinking can amplify these issues and lead to more severe problems. It is important for parents, teachers, and other adults to be vigilant in recognizing the signs of negative thinking in young people and to provide support and guidance.

Negative thinking poses to be a difficult habit to break, but it is possible. With the right strategies, individuals can learn to break free from the cycle of negative thinking and create a more positive outlook on life.

Breaking free from negative thinking can lead to improved mental and physical health, more productive work habits, and a better overall quality of life.

Negative thinking can have a detrimental effect on the mental and physical health of teenagers. Thinking negatively can lead to feelings of low self-esteem and depression, which can then lead to physical symptoms such as headaches, fatigue, and gastrointestinal distress. It can also lead to an increase in stress, which can further worsen physical and mental health. Negative thinking can also lead to difficulty sleeping, poor concentration, and poor academic performance.

Negative thinking can also have a profound effect on a teenager's social life. Teens who think negatively may be more likely to be socially isolated and to have difficulty forming meaningful relationships. They may be more likely to engage in risky behaviors such as drug and alcohol use, and may be more likely to experience negative peer pressure.

Negative thinking can also lead to a decrease in a teenager's motivation. Teens who think negatively may lack the motivation to pursue their goals, may not take advantage of available opportunities, and may become apathetic about their future.

Negative thinking can lead to a decrease in a teenager's overall happiness and well-being. Teens who think negatively may be more likely to experience feelings of sadness and hopelessness, and may be more likely to engage in self-destructive behaviors. It can also lead to an increase in self-doubt, which can further worsen mental and physical health.

Strategy 1:

Recognize Your Negative Thoughts

Negative thoughts can be powerful, intrusive and hard to shake. They can undermine our self-esteem, make us feel anxious, or make us doubt our abilities. Recognizing our negative thoughts is an important part of managing them.

Negative thoughts often come in the form of self-criticism, such as "I'm not good enough" or "I'm a failure". Other times they may be more general, such as "nothing ever works out for me" or "I'm always the one who gets left behind". Whatever form they take, negative thoughts can be damaging and can lead to a cycle of self-sabotaging behavior.

The first step to recognizing our negative thoughts is to become aware of them. This can be difficult, because we often don't recognize our thoughts as negative until it's too late. To help us become more aware, it can be helpful to practice mindfulness or to keep a journal of our thoughts.

Once we've become aware of our negative thoughts, the next step is to challenge them. This can be done by asking ourselves questions such as: "Is this thought really true?" or "How can I look at this situation in a different way?". We can also use positive self-talk to counter our negative thoughts.

We can swap our negative thoughts with more positive ones. This doesn't mean we have to ignore our negative thoughts altogether, but rather that we can choose to focus on the positive aspects of a situation or to remind ourselves of our strengths and abilities.

Recognizing our negative thoughts is an important part of managing them. By becoming aware of our negative thoughts, challenging them and replacing them with more positive ones, we can take back control and start to feel better about ourselves and our lives.

An example of a negative thought could be "I always fail at everything I do." This type of thinking can be incredibly damaging to our self-esteem, as it paints a negative picture of ourselves and our capabilities. To challenge this thought, we can ask ourselves questions such as "What evidence do I have to support this thought?" or "What have I achieved lately that I'm proud of?". We can also use positive self-talk such as "I may have made mistakes in the past, but I can also learn from them and move forward". Finally, we can replace the negative thought with a more positive one such as "I am capable and strong, and I can achieve my goals."

Strategy 2:

Challenge Your Thoughts

Challenge Your Thoughts (CYT) is an effective way of stopping negative thinking as a teenager. It encourages young people to become more aware of their thoughts and to take control of them. CYT helps teens to recognize the power of their thoughts and to understand how they can influence their behaviour and feelings.

The first step in CYT is to become aware of the negative thoughts. This means noticing when they come up, and understanding why they are happening. Once teens are aware of their negative thoughts, they can begin to challenge them. This involves questioning the thoughts and looking for evidence that supports or refutes them. For example, if a teen is feeling down and has a negative thought saying "I can't do anything right", they can challenge this thought by looking for evidence that this is not true.

The next step in CYT is to replace the negative thought with a positive one. This involves focusing on the good things about oneself, and shifting the focus away from the negative. For example, if a teen is feeling down and has a negative thought saying "I'm not good enough", they can replace this thought with "I am capable of great things". This helps to shift the focus away from the negative and towards the positive.

The final step in CYT is to take action. This involves finding ways to cope with the negative thoughts and feelings. This can be done through activities such as deep breathing, exercise, journaling, or talking to a trusted friend or family member. It is important to remember that it is okay to feel anxious and sad sometimes, but it is important to find healthy ways to cope.

Overall, CYT is an effective way of stopping negative thinking as a teenager. It helps teens to recognize the power of their thoughts and to take control of them. By becoming aware of the negative thoughts, challenging them, and replacing them with positive ones, teens can learn how to manage their thoughts and feelings in a healthy way.

Being aware of your thoughts will help you to become more mindful and to recognize the power of your thoughts and feelings. With practice, this will help you to manage negative thoughts and feelings in a healthy way.

CYT is a helpful method of dealing with negative thinking because it encourages teens to take an active role in managing their thoughts and feelings. It helps them to become aware of their thoughts, challenge them, and replace them with positive ones. With practice, teens can learn to manage their thoughts and feelings in a healthy way, leading to improved mental health.

Benefits of CYT include improved self-esteem and self-confidence, as well as improved emotional regulation and problem solving skills. It can also help teens to become more aware of their emotions, allowing them to better understand themselves and their reactions to different situations.

Strategy 3:
Reframe Your Thoughts

Reframing your thoughts is an important skill for teenagers to learn in order to prevent negative thinking. It involves replacing negative or irrational thoughts with more realistic and positive ones. Reframing your thoughts is a way to change the way you look at a situation, allowing you to take control of your thoughts and emotions.

When faced with a difficult situation, it's easy to get overwhelmed and think negatively. Negative thoughts can lead to feelings of depression, anxiety, and stress. Reframing your thoughts can help you to respond to the situation in a more constructive way.

To reframe your thoughts, start by recognizing the negative thought. Acknowledge that it is there, but don't dwell on it or give it too much power. Instead, focus on finding an alternative way of looking at the situation. Ask yourself questions such as: Is this really as bad as I think it is? What can I do to make this better? What are some positive aspects of this situation?

Once you have identified more positive thoughts, focus on them and allow them to become your focus. This can help to reduce the power of the negative ones. It is also important to be kind to yourself. Remind yourself that everyone makes mistakes and has bad days, and that it's okay to feel negative emotions occasionally.

It's important to practice reframing your thoughts regularly. This will help you to become more aware of the negative thoughts that come into your head, and to be able to respond to them more constructively. With practice, you can learn to challenge and replace negative thoughts more quickly, allowing you to move on to more positive and productive thinking.

Reframing your thoughts is an important skill for teenagers to learn as it can help them to better manage difficult situations and reduce the power of negative thinking. With practice, reframing your thoughts can become a habit, allowing you to take control of your thoughts and emotions and lead a more positive and productive life.

As a teenager you can reframe your thoughts by:

1. Recognizing the negative thought: Acknowledge that it is there, but don't dwell on it or give it too much power.

2. Finding an alternative way of looking at the situation: Ask yourself questions such as: Is this really as bad as I think it is? What do I do to make this better? What are some encouraging aspects of this situation?

3. Focusing on positive thoughts: Once you have identified more positive thoughts, focus on them and allow them to become your focus. This can help to reduce the power of the negative ones.

4. Being kind to yourself: Remind yourself that everyone makes mistakes

and has bad days, and that it's okay to feel negative emotions occasionally.

5. Practicing regularly: It's important to practice reframing your thoughts regularly. This will help you to become more aware of the negative thoughts that come into your head, and to be able to respond to them more constructively.

Benefits of reframing your thoughts as a teenager include:

1. Improved mental health: Reframing your thoughts can help you to better manage difficult situations and reduce the power of negative thinking.

2. Increased resilience: With practice, reframing your thoughts can become a habit, allowing you to take control of

your thoughts and emotions and lead a more positive and productive life.

3. Improved communication: Reframing your thoughts can also help you to communicate better with others, as it allows you to better understand their perspective and respond to them in a more positive way.

Overall, reframing your thoughts is an important skill for teenagers to learn as it can help to reduce the power of negative thinking and lead to improved mental health, increased resilience and better communication. With practice, you can learn to challenge and replace negative thoughts more quickly, allowing you to move on to more positive and productive thinking.

Strategy 4:
Practice Self-Care

Practicing self-care is a key way of stopping negative thinking as a teenager. Self-care is defined as any activity we do deliberately to take care of our mental, emotional, and physical health. It involves activities that nurture our well-being, such as eating healthy foods, exercising, getting enough sleep, and avoiding substance abuse.

When it comes to stopping negative thinking, self-care is key. Negative thoughts can be debilitating and can lead to a cycle of destructive behavior. Self-care can help break this cycle and provide a positive alternative to negative thinking.

One way to practice self-care is to take time out of your day to do something that you enjoy. You can either choose to be listening to music or going for a walk, or reading a book. Taking the time to do something that you enjoy can help to reduce stress and bring your mind back to a more positive place.

Another way to practice self-care is to practice mindfulness. Mindfulness is the practice of being conscious of your thoughts, feelings, and sensations without judgment. It can help you be more aware of your inner dialogue and give you the space to recognize and challenge negative thoughts. It can also help you to recognize and appreciate your own strengths and abilities.

It is important to talk to someone about your negative thoughts and feelings. Talking to a trusted adult or a mental health professional can help you to better understand your negative thoughts and feelings and can help you to develop strategies to manage and reduce them.

Practicing self-care is an important way to stop negative thinking as a teenager. It can help to reduce stress, provide a positive alternative to negative thinking, and help to develop better coping strategies. Taking the time to practice self-care can make all the difference in managing and reducing negative thoughts and feelings.

Teenagers can practice self care in the following ways:

1. Eating a healthy, balanced diet – Eating a healthy diet can help to reduce stress and provide essential nutrients that can help to improve mental health and wellbeing.

2. Exercise – Exercise is an effective way to reduce stress and improve mental health. It can also provide an outlet for frustration and negative thoughts.

3. Get enough sleep – Getting enough sleep is indispensable for physical and mental health. It can help to reduce stress and improve mood.

4. Connect with friends and family – Spending time with friends and family can help to reduce stress and provide a positive environment to talk about your thoughts and feelings.

5. Pursue your passions – Pursuing activities that you are passionate about can help to provide a positive focus and distract from negative thoughts.

6. Spend time in nature – Being in nature can help to reduce stress and provide a sense of calm.

7. Meditate – Meditation can help to reduce stress and provide a sense of calm.

8. Practice gratitude – Practicing gratitude can help to redirect your focus from negative thoughts to positive ones.

9. Talk to someone – Talking to a trusted adult or a mental health professional can help to better understand your negative thoughts and

feelings and can help to develop strategies to manage and reduce them.

10. Take time for yourself – Taking time for yourself to do something that you enjoy can help to reduce stress and bring your mind back to a more positive place.

Practicing self care can be beneficial in many ways, and can help to reduce stress and provide a positive alternative to negative thinking. It can also help to develop better coping strategies and provide a sense of calm. Taking the time to practice self-care can make all the difference in managing and reducing negative thoughts and feelings.

Strategy 5:

Talk to Someone

Talking to someone is an effective way for teenagers to stop negative thinking. Negative thinking can lead to feelings of low self-esteem, feelings of worthlessness, and depression. By talking to someone, teenagers can learn how to better manage their thoughts and feelings and develop healthier coping skills.

Talking to someone can provide a sense of understanding and support. For example, talking to a friend or family member can allow a teenager to express their feelings and get feedback about their situation. This can help them to gain perspective and insight into how their negative thinking is impacting their life. Additionally, talking to someone can provide a safe space for teens to be open and honest about their thoughts, fears, and worries without fear of judgement.

Talking to someone can also provide teens with the opportunity to learn specific techniques to help them manage their negative thinking. For example, they can learn coping strategies such as positive self-talk, relaxation techniques, and mindfulness. These strategies can help teens to reframe their thoughts, recognize the impact of their thoughts and feelings, and develop more positive perspectives.

Talking to someone can also help teenagers to get to the root cause of their negative thinking. By exploring the underlying causes, teens can gain insight into how their thoughts and feelings are connected to their life experiences and can learn how to better manage their thoughts and feelings.

Talking to someone can also provide teens with a sense of connection and belonging. By talking to someone, teens can learn that they are not alone in their struggles and that there are people who understand and care about their well-being.

Overall, talking to someone is an effective way for teenagers to stop negative thinking. By talking to someone, teens can gain insight, learn coping strategies, explore the root cause of their negative thinking, and find a sense of connection and belonging.

Talking to someone is beneficial in stopping negative thinking because it allows individuals to express their feelings and receive feedback, learn specific techniques to manage their negative thinking, and gain insight into the root cause of their negative thinking. Additionally, talking to someone provides a sense of understanding and support, and can help individuals to feel connected and less alone in their struggles.

Strategy 6:

Monitor Your Progress

Monitoring progress is an important part of managing negative thinking as a teenager. It involves paying attention to your thoughts, feelings, and behaviors in relation to your goals and objectives. By taking a moment to pause and reflect on how you are doing, you can become aware of your successes and challenges in achieving your goals. It can be difficult to monitor your progress, especially when faced with challenges and obstacles. However, by taking the time to track and reflect on your progress, you can gain insight into your current state of mind and identify areas where you can make positive changes.

When it comes to managing negative thinking, monitoring your progress can be a powerful tool. It can help you recognize when you are engaging in negative thoughts and feelings, as well as when you are making positive progress towards achieving your goals. For example, if you are feeling overwhelmed or stuck in a rut, take a few moments to pause and reflect on what you have accomplished in the past week or month. By doing this, you can identify areas of success and determine what you need to work on in order to make further progress.

Monitoring your progress can also help you recognize patterns in your thinking and behavior. For example, if you find that you are often engaging in negative self-talk or ruminating on past mistakes, pay attention to when and why these thoughts are occurring. This can help you become aware of the underlying causes of your negative thoughts and feelings, allowing you to develop strategies to address them. Additionally, monitoring your progress can help you recognize when you have made positive changes in your life, allowing you to gain confidence in your ability to continue making progress.

Overall, monitoring your progress is an important way of managing negative thinking as a teenager. By taking the time to pause and reflect on your progress, you can become aware of both your successes and challenges. This can help you gain insight into your current state of mind and develop strategies to address the underlying causes of your negative thinking. Additionally, it can help you gain confidence in your ability to make positive changes in your life.

Strategy 7:

Take Action

Negative thinking is a common problem among teenagers. It can lead to feelings of sadness, anxiety, and low self-esteem. Fortunately, there are ways to combat negative thinking and take action to combat it.

First, it is important to identify the source of negative thinking. This can be done by recognizing any patterns in the thoughts or feelings that are present. Once it is identified, it can be addressed by understanding why it is occurring and by making changes to the environment or situation if necessary.

Once the source of negative thinking is identified, it is important to take action to combat it. This can include engaging in positive self-talk, challenging unhelpful thoughts, and developing coping skills. Positive self-talk is a way of talking to yourself in a positive and supportive way. Challenging unhelpful thoughts involves examining the evidence for and against the thought and determining if it is true. Developing coping skills can include learning how to relax, how to manage stress, and how to manage emotions.

In addition to taking action to combat negative thinking, it is important to develop healthy habits to maintain a positive mindset. These can include getting enough sleep, eating nutritious foods, exercising regularly, and taking time to relax and de-stress.

As teenagers, it can be easy to get bogged down in negative thinking. It can be difficult to break out of this cycle, leaving us feeling helpless and hopeless. However, there are steps we can take to help us move away from negative thinking and towards a more positive frame of mind.

The first step is to recognize when our thoughts are negative. This can be difficult, as negative thoughts can become so ingrained in our thinking that we don't even realize how much we are engaging in them. It is important to take a step back and observe our thoughts, so that we can recognize when we are engaging in negative thinking.

Once we have identified our negative thoughts, we need to take action to stop them. This can be achieved in a variety of ways. We can challenge the negative thoughts by asking ourselves questions such as 'Is this really true?' or 'What is the evidence for this thought?' We can also engage in activities such as physical exercise, meditation, or journaling to help us focus on the present moment and take our mind off our negative thoughts.

It can also be helpful to reach out to a trusted adult or friend for support. Talking to someone else can help us to gain perspective and get a different point of view on the situation. This can help to put our negative thoughts into context and make them seem less overwhelming.

It is important to practice self-compassion. We can be our own worst critics, and it is important to remember that we are all human and make mistakes. Instead of being hard on ourselves, we can focus on self-care and being kind to ourselves.

By recognizing our negative thoughts, taking action to stop them, and practicing self-compassion, we can take steps to break the cycle of negative thinking. This can help us to feel more optimistic and in control of our lives, and can ultimately lead to greater happiness and wellbeing.

Conclusion

As a teenager, negative thinking can be a hard habit to break, but with the right strategies in place, it doesn't have to be an overwhelming and insurmountable task. The first step is to become aware of the negative thoughts and to recognize that they are not helpful or productive. Once this is done, replacing the negative thoughts with positive ones can be challenging but can be done with practice. Developing self-confidence and self-esteem, using positive self-talk, and engaging in activities that bring joy can help to reduce the frequency of negative thinking. Additionally, creating a support system of positive people, talking to a counselor or therapist, and understanding that negative thoughts are often based on fear can be beneficial in helping to stop negative thinking. Finally, learning to be more mindful and practicing relaxation techniques can help to reduce the intensity and frequency of negative thinking. Although it may take some time and effort to break the habit of negative thinking, it is achievable and can lead to a more fulfilling and enjoyable life.

Dealing with negative thinking is essential because it can profoundly affect a person's mental health and well-being. By using the strategies outlined in this book, teenagers can begin to take control of their negative thoughts and lead a more positive and fulfilling life.

Stay mentally sound by dealing with negative thinking. The danger of negative thinking can be prevented by applying the strategies mentioned in this book. With these strategies, teenagers can break the cycle of negative thinking and lead a life full of positivity and joy.